Sincerely Yours,
A Black Man

By: Darryl Johnson

Copyright © 2022 by Darryl Johnson
All rights reserved. This book or any portion
thereof may not be reproduced or used in any
manner whatsoever without the express
written permission of the publisher except for
the use of brief quotations in a book review.
Printed in the United States of America
First Printing, 2023
ISBN **979-8-9875359-0-5**
Djohnson73188@outlook.com

FOREWORD

Time brings about change. It's inevitable; but often change makes you think: Where was the ball dropped or how did this come to pass?

After having a conversation with a few black women, they raised concern when they said, "Women don't feel appreciated by men, Black Women don't feel appreciated by our Black Men!"

Being taken back by their comments, SINCERELY YOURS, A BLACK MAN came to be.

SINCERELY YOURS, A BLACK MAN is a book of poems dedicated to Women (Especially BLACK Women) from the thoughts and perspective of a Black Man to show love and appreciation.

It is also a reminder to women of who you are and how remarkable you are.

Though there is more to be done, let this be a step in the right direction.

~Darryl Johnson~

Table of Contents

B.L.A.C.K W.O.M.A.N 1

YOU ARE MAGIC 4

Essential to Life 7

Queen 9

Unequivocal 12

In·perfection 14

A Dozen Roses 18

P.S.A. 20

Blessing 23

Sunshine 25

Divine Connection 27

Rhythm and Blues 29

Absolute Elegance 31

Dark Skinned 33

Light Skinned 35

More Than Enough 37

Sultry 40

Homage 43

Courage 45

Ethereal 49

Conferrer 51

As You Are	53
Arise	56
Sensational	59
Remember Your Worth	63
Astounding	66
Here I Stand	70
Graceful	73
Rebirth of a Queen	76
My Apologies	78
Treasure	82
Refuge	84
These Eyes	88

B.L.A.C.K W.O.M.A.N

Beautiful

The melanin of your skin is envied by those who don't possess it naturally. The curves of your body entice the mind and seduce the thoughts of anyone that gets to look at you. You walk with a fierceness that demands attention.........

Deserves attention.........

It has already been foretold, of how beautiful you are. You are echoed in the Song of Songs. The one that is hated by most because she naturally has what everyone else wants. The Sun that breathes light into life.

Loving

Love is in your nature. Passion exudes from your pores and attracts people to you. The warmth of your soul attaches them to the essence that is you. The heart you possess nourishes the soul and fills others with compassion. You feed your kindness to whoever is hungry for it and embrace everyone with open arms. Peace is the overwhelming feeling that covers those that hear your voice. You silence the world that declares war against you with a simple stroke of your touch. A kiss from you can heal all things as if it were filled with the touch of God. Your love is everlasting and unwavering. It's the cure to what is evil in this world.

Astonishing

You embody excellence. You complement anything and give it new life. You enhance everything you touch and add beauty to anything around you. You are the true reflection of the beauty in this world. In fact, you are the truest form of beauty in this world.

Compelling

You are the best part of the world. You empower and inspire the people around you to reach pinnacles unimaginable. You create confidence and instill value in our youth. The reflection you see daily is the most influential aspect of life in any way you can fathom,

Knowledgeable

You are the greatest source of wisdom one can find. You counsel the heavy minds and are a nurse to the broken hearted. You speak with a voice that can change a boy into a man, if he listens. You are the teacher of life in an abundance of ways.

B.L.A.C.K. WOMAN,

You are what the world is blind to, but the most beautiful sight to see. The closest thing we have on this Earth to Heaven. You are the reason men become who they are. The reason our daughters know their true worth and our sons know how to respect women. There are many words to describe you, Beautiful, Loving, Astonishing, Compelling and Knowledgeable are just a few. The true definition of beauty is defined by what's inside of you. You are mother to the world. You are invaluable, irreplaceable, incomparable and inimitable. The Queen of the hearts of many and the royalty that stands alongside of her people. Continue to be the magnificent being you are.

With Love and Adoration,

A Black Man

YOU ARE MAGIC

*Y*outhful is what your spirit is. It's full of laughter and energy that can easily spread for miles on end.

*O*mnipotence is not only what you display, but what you were manifested to express. Giving a living example of what lies in the heavens.

*U*nfeigned with every action and every gesture you make. Every word that's ever been spoken from your lips tastes sweet.

*A*ltruistic in many ways, especially in the lives of those you love and care for. Sacrificing yourself effortlessly to elevate the confidence of those around you and uplift their spirits.

*R*esplendent in the eyes of those that get to see you every day. They understand that your true wealth seeps from the depths of your heart and that you are invaluable.

*E*nlivening life; making every minute, of every hour, of every day worthwhile. There is not a day that goes by where you are not a miracle and a blessing to us all.

Magnanimous, especially to those who have done you wrong and that are undeserving of your forgiveness. You encompass the word and are a living testament to it.

An Affable lover and friend. Allowing the burden of life to be lighter than a feather and healing wounds that run deeper than the eyes can see.

Genial by nature......supportive and resilient. All qualities that embody perfection, redefine beauty, and symbolize strength, you possess.

Inspirational and motivational to the world. Gravitating everyone towards the light that shines from a simple smile. Encouraging those that have doubt or disbelief in themselves. Giving them hope and a perspective that they have never seen.

Compassionate to those who have troubles. Sympathetic to the pain you see in others. More than a shoulder for them to cry on in their time of need.

Now extract the bold letter of every paragraph and it will tell you exactly what you are.

YOU ARE MAGIC!!!

You are the greatest and most precious gift that life has to offer. This is just a friendly reminder that you are appreciated and loved.

Sincerely Yours,

A Black Man

Essential to Life

Understanding is an essential part of life and development.

To be the best form of man I can be....

I need to understand a woman and the value she possesses.

Going back to the beginning....

The bible says that Adam was given the authority to name the creatures in the world,

As he did, he found none of them worthy of being a suitable companion for him in the world.

So God placed him in a deep sleep and created woman from his rib.

We know this story, yet some of us men remain asleep on you.

Some still don't recognize the greatness that resides inside of you.

Some don't realize your importance and true value.

You are the foundation on which love is built.

The backbone of every man that he didn't know he had.

You are the personification of water.

Necessary to allow life to flow.

You are the air that is needed for the soul to breathe.

You are the representation of God on this Earth,

Because you take seeds and give them life.

Bringing a joy to the world that cannot exist without you.

Without you I would not be here,

So I open my eyes and heart in reverence to you to say thank you

And I see you!

Sincerely Yours,

A Black Man

Queen

Behold the beauty that is she

Magnificent in every facet of the word.

Created by God, so there could be divinity within the world.

Bringing humility to the arrogant,

And giving confidence to the coy.

There is no crown that won't fit you

No pedestal that is too high for you.

You and your aura uplift everything that surrounds you.

You are the sun that feeds the flowers to bloom.

You are the light of the moon.

The better half of any union.

The serenity within the chaos.

It's astounding that so much good can be capsulated into such a resplendent individual

I am humbled to be able to be in your presence

You are the perfect leader,

Never letting a single soul diminish your volition.

Having the poise to let others lead....

And still maintaining control in the background.

When necessary, you take the lead and control what need to be handled.

You have been royalty since birth.

Lineage only continues because you exist.

The reason a prince becomes king is because he has you.

The reason legacies even last.

You are the greatest gift to man

And the greatest gift to the world

Even without a crown

You are always and forever

A QUEEN!!!

Sincerely Yours,

A Black Man

Unequivocal

You are the physical manifestation of Heaven on Earth.

Walking with much grace and poise.

Stealing the attention of everyone whose path you cross.

With every step you take,

You walk with elegance,

Step with purpose and strength.

Your melanin is Godly!!!!

Possessing the power of the sun in your skin.

Radiating warmth in every direction.

Enviable by all yet envious of none.

So bright that you don't cast a shadow.

You have your flaws,

But there is no mistaking that you were made to perfection.

You have no equal,

Yet remain humble to show your true nature.

You are the anomaly.

The embodiment of everything magnificent.

Majestic in all your ways.

Without you,

This world is destitute.

I'm forever grateful for your presence.

Sincerely Yours,

A Black Man

In·perfection

If you pay attention to what's being said,

You will come to find that the most egregious things are said about the most "perfect" people.

They stereotype you because they can't stand their own reflection.

Their "criticism" is just symbolic to their ignorance and envy.

Calling you angry, uneducated, loud, and lazy

How dare them have the audacity to speak this way.

You are one of, if not the most unappreciated being that exists.

Being a minority in more ways than one.

If anyone has a right to be angry, it's you!

But your passion and unwillingness to be susceptible to bullshit is misconstrued.

I'd beg you to stay true to you.

Because you don't need to conform to their views.

Uneducated?

How can someone fix their lips to speak such foolishness?

Do they not understand the influence and impact that you have on history?

You are the foundation of knowledge in the world.

The lessons you teach are embedded in the mind, engraved in the spirit and entrenched in the soul.

Even without a degree,

You are looked upon for your wisdom.

Loud?

You have been silenced for too long.

Placed on the back burner by your oppressor

And your "protector" has left you with unhealable scars.

Your voice needs to be heard.

Demands to be heard

It's melodic and I'm glad that you found it.

Lazy?

How could you be lazy?

Carrying the weight of the world on your shoulders.

Being everything,

For everyone,

At all times,

It's exhausting.

Yet you carry that burden with class and poise.

Mothering all the children of the world,

And too frequently.... having to father your own alone.

I see that you are tired

So rest up,

You deserve to.

With everything they find wrong with you....
You embrace and make it wonderful

Because people often find flaws....

In·perfection

Which You Are!

Sincerely Yours,

A Black Man

A Dozen Roses

One rose to you for your pretty smile
And waking the world up with your warmth.

A Second for the love you so eloquently speak
into the ones that surround you.
Giving hope and faith to those who need it.

The third is for the pain you endure.
Have to endure,
Had to endure.
I apologize for you ever having to feel that.

The fourth is for your patience.
Holding still while surrounded with commotion.

The fifth rose is for kindness.
Continuously caring for others, more than you
do for yourself

A sixth is for your faith.
The faith that you hold on to that helps you
push through
And the faith you give to make people believe.

The seventh is for your ability to love.
Unconditional and unwavering love.
The truest form of love that ever existed.

The eighth is for your nurturing nature.

The ability to not only feed the belly,
But your ability to manifest a seed into a son,
and a dream into reality.

The ninth is for your loyalty.
Standing firm on the foundation that was built
in your relationships.
Never folding under pressure from others,
Nor leaving when faced with misfortune.

The tenth is for your understanding.
Knowing how to calm the storm of the mind
And ease the pain of those misunderstood

An eleventh is for all of your support.
Whether it be financially, mentally or physically
Doing whatever is necessary to ensure the
outcome is always positive.

A twelfth is purely because you are a special
person

A dozen roses for a Simply Amazing Woman

Sincerely Yours,

A Black Man

P.S.A.

May I have your attention please,

Whatever you are doing is not more pertinent than what I have to say right now.

Let me have your undivided attention and focus as you read the words on this page.

I dedicate this one to you,

The ones who are not loved enough.

The ones whose heartbeats make the world turn.

Today,

In this very moment,

You will be eternally recognized.

These words may not hold much weight to you because they are coming from someone you may not know,

Or someone you may not want to hear them from.

But they do need to be heard, and I hope they are felt.

Being able to see you is the best part of my day.

There is something about your smile that restores the light in my soul.

Being able to see you automatically makes a bad day, the best day ever.

I often wish that moment would never cease or fade,

But last just a little bit longer.

I mat not know you personally,

Yet I want to thank you from the bottom of my heart.

Thank you for being unapologetically you.

I pity the men and women who overlook you.

They are foolish to not see the value in such a gem, because it may have a few flaws.

They fail to see your strength because they are blinded by their own weakness.

I want you to understand that I recognize your greatness.

I can see the greatness that you manifest into the world.

I AM NOT BLIND TO YOU.

Your speech rivals those of the past.

Encouraging and enlightening the spirits of whoever hears your voice.

Empowering men to strive for greatness,

Striking fear in the heart of those that oppose.

Your words are one of many weapons in your arsenal,

They carry enough power to bring war or deliver peace.

Your sound brings solace to the soul.

And will forever remain echoed in my mind.

I hope you realize, just as much as I do, how wonderful you are.

I pray these words touch a piece of you, and bring you some semblance of peace

And appreciation

Sincerely yours,

A Black Man.

<u>Blessing</u>

How blessed am I to be able to hold such a beautiful sight in my eyes.
I am privileged to hear your words
And humbled that you deem me worthy.
It's unbelievable that such a majestic figure graces' us with her presence.

Have you ever just stopped in a moment,
Stood in front of the mirror,
And reflected on just how simply amazing you are?

Have you ever shown reverence to yourself?
Appreciated the person you truly are?

If you haven't,
Then you have committed a crime against yourself.
Sometimes, the best gratification one can receive is from oneself.

Let me reinforce what should already be known among the masses.
There is nothing in this world that is quite like you.

You are the perfectly packaged gift that was given by God to the world.

You are the ultimate enhancer.
Making pretty be beautiful.
Transforming intelligence into wisdom.
Turning fear into fortitude
And so much more.

You are the reason…
The reason I smile,
The reason I Walk,
And the reason I stand as the man I am.

Thank God and you for your existence

I love you,

Sincerely Yours,
A Black Man

<u>Sunshine</u>

Sunshine

You are the brightest part of any day,
No matter your skin complexion.
You are the heat,
That warms the soul.
You are a true hearts reflection.
Your beauty is undeniable and incomparable.
Bliss is felt most when your presence is near.
Darkness dissipates from the light you bring.
You are the abundance of joy,
The feeling of hope,
The translation of love,
And the personification of perfection
Combined into one being.
You are not only the giver of life,
But you expound it.
You give meaning and purpose to the existence of me.

Let your rays forever flourish,
And disperse a spectrum of brightness throughout time.

You are magnanimous
You are Powerful
You are a Loved

And you are appreciated

Sincerely Yours,
A Black Man

Divine Connection

The only way I can live forever.......
Is through you,
Developing my seed,
Upholding and uplifting my name.
The words you speak about me,
Echo in history,
To keep a record of my legacy....
Of who I am.

The hierarchy of the family,
Is Christ, Husband, Wife, and Child(ren).
As the Husband,
My responsibilities are said to be,
to provide, protect, and lead.
The Wife,
To comfort, teach and nurture.
And that you always do.

You are the Connection.
The reason I have deep relationships.
I am bonded by God with you.

You are what I have always prayed for.
The answer to my call.

You teach me through love and understanding,
That I am not alone,
And that I am connected to this world in a deep capacity.

You are not only my rib,
You are also my third eye.
My roots in this world that connects me with nature.
The booster of my spiritual connection with God.

I pray and thank God for creating you for me.

I thank you for staying beside me,
Tapping into my soul,
And giving me vision for things I was blind to.

I love you,
And I am forever indebted to you

Sincerely Yours,
A Black Man

Rhythm and Blues

Melodies of you
Have been heard around the world.
Sentiments of love and lust,
Have danced through time.
Finger snaps to catch the rhythm,
Sounding like a quick kiss of your lips.

Beats were created to watch you move.
Feet hitting the ground,
Replicating the sound of bongo drums.
Shaking your assets in seductive fashion.

Do you hear the sounds of those horns?
They are screaming out to you.
Wanting to catch your attention.
Calling out to you,
Wanting you to feel them,
As much as they do you.

Those high notes,
Add depth to the moment.
Just as you do.
Gliding across the sky,
As we dance on the moon.

Slow Jams…

Oh, those slow jams,
Were made for You and I,
As we come closer.
Moving to the same tune.
Our hearts are in harmony
As the words from our song play.

You're the perfect ballad.
A symphony,
That's kept sacredly,
Throughout history.
A song that's beautiful whether it's
instrumental
Or acapella.

You are a classic
And I love the music we make

Sincerely Yours.
A Black Man

Absolute Elegance

Any woman can be beautiful,

But it takes more than exterior physique to be elegant.

To have a smile as bright as the night stars,

Skin as flawless as the creator himself,

With curves that flow like the ocean.

Not even the goddess Aphrodite can compare.

All of that is well, but true beauty will never make eternal blithe.

You still possess so much more.

Your beauty,

Captures my eyes every moment I catch even the slightest glimpse of you.

Your words,

Grabbed my ears as if you were singing me a melody that was only meant for me to hear.

Your actions……. so genuine, seize more than my heart,

And something that feels deeper than my soul.

It's astounding that one person can do one thing…………. so simple, yet still has an everlasting impact on your world.

I say these things so that my heart can show you the love that it's wanted to express since the first time a thought of you invaded my mind.

To call you beautiful would not only be an understatement,

But an insult as well.

You are excellence

And Perfection.

You embrace elegance,

Which is deeper than beauty in my eyes.

Sincerely Yours,

A Black Man

Dark Skinned

What a site to behold!
Enriched with sunlight to produce black excellence in every way.
My favorite piece of chocolate that Hersey can't replicate.
But I do wish they could duplicate

They don't understand your depth.
How rooted you are in this world.
Your skin is the color of dirt,
Yet, they don't realize you are the soil that helps this world grow.
Your color is the foundation of the best flavors.
The chocolate that soothes and comforts
Or they must not know that vanilla comes from a brown plant too.
Don't that taste sweet?

Do you know how much they envy you?
Degrading your looks because they don't have what you have.
Calling your hair nappy
Because they don't understand its strength.
Trying to make a mockery of your skin tone,

Because theirs is so bland.

Every insult they throw at you,
Take it.
And hold it with pride.
Because they fear what you possess,
And what they lack inside.

Your skin is earth toned.
That means its strong,
And the foundation on which we stand.

Your Black is Beautiful
Your Melanin is Magic
Never forget that.

With love and appreciation,

Sincerely Yours,
A Black Man

Light Skinned

You look like honey,
And just as sweet.
Love from you,
Is such a treat.
Like a dollop of caramel.

You are often judged cruelly,
People thinking you are uppity
Or just flat out bougie.
Always thinking,
"She thinks she's better than someone because she light skinned"

That just goes to show,
How little they know,
Because you were already made better.
Even before your skin tone was even a factor in the equation.

It's no secret that you are envied.
Even by those that should embrace you.
Though they hate on you,
They wish they could have you
And wish they could be you.

You were carefully crafted,

With sophistication and elegance.
The standard by which beauty is measured.
A tan can't replicate the kiss that the sun left on you.

To see you in the sunlight,
Glistening,
Your radiance, penetrating the eyes that behold you.

Remember your worth,
your skin tone is matched with items of the highest value,
Yet those items still aren't comparable to your merit.

You are blended to perfection.

A true representation of how beautiful the world can be,
If we come together

Thank you for being you,
And being a place of warmth in cold world.

Sincerely Yours,
A Black Man

More Than Enough

"Why am I not enough for you?"
"Am I too fat?"
"Am I too skinny?"
"Am I not that pretty?"
"What is it about me that makes you treat me this way?"

These are a few questions that plague your mind when you're mistreated and unloved.
Self-doubt corrupts the mind
And evicts the confidence that once resided there.
Leaving you with feelings of emptiness.
Planting seeds of lies,
That's watered with his words
To make thoughts of unworthiness grow deep within.

Let's pause for a moment............

Take a deep breathe.............

And examine the truth in this instance.

YOU ARE NOT THE REASON FOR HIS TRANSGRESSION!!!

The reason he cannot be honest with you,
Is because he cannot be honest with himself.
Accountability is an area where many fall short.
Not fully comprehending the role they play.
Maturity hasn't fully set in
And self-reflection isn't something we want to face.

Today I pray we do better,
For you are the greatest gift.
I hope we are no longer blinded to your beauty,
But can see who you truly are.
I pray we are more forthcoming with how we feel,
As opposed to hiding behind the cowardice of infidelity
or deception of "happiness"

Let it be known,
You are more than enough
The fulfillment of every desire,

The greatest source of enrichment.
More deserving than those unworthy
A gift from the Most High

Sincerely Yours,
A Black Man.

Sultry

My God My God!!!

What a sight to behold

I don't know what you have done to me,

But my body has lost all control.

Hypnotized by the sway of your hips.

Lusting over the lusciousness of your lips.

Damn I see you!!!!

How could anyone not?

That silhouette speaks volumes.

Your simple gestures look exotic.

You pleasure all senses with a mere whisper.

An innocent hug brings erotic thoughts to the minds of those you touch.

Being nubile is an understatement.

You cause processions and stand stills when you are in ones view.

Arousing the mind, body and soul

Uncontrollable urges pulsating through the mind,

Extremities sweating with excitement and anticipation.

Genitalia remaining not so private.

Wanting to taste the passion of your core,

And the best parts of you.
The way you move makes my heart skip beats.

It's easy for someone to find themselves

Lost in your essence.

Drowning in the pool of your pretty brown eyes.

You accentuate life's pleasantries.

Making diamonds shine brighter.

Colors more vibrant,

And moments into unforgettable memories.

You are more than a covet.

You entice a desire so strong,

That the feelings transform into a promise of a lifetime love,

A covenant.

Sexy isn't what you are,

It's what you define!

Sincerely Yours,
A Black Man

Homage

There is nothing better than the love of A Black Woman!

The way she nurtures the soul is unmatched.
Feeding knowledge to the hungry mind.
Re-energizing the body of those who are tired of trying.
Comforting the heart from the agony it once knew,
Rehydrating those who thirst for love.

How?
How is it possible that you elevate Heaven?
Every voice that can hold a note,
Should sing praises to your name.

The power of your tongue molds boys into men,
Girls into beautiful women.
You inspire greatness,
Instill value,
And promote growth in all aspects of life.

The greatest healer known to man.
From a simple kiss,

To a gentle whisper,
You make everything feel better.

You are the peace in a chaotic world.
The balance to all instability.

To you, I am forever grateful and appreciative.

Sincerely Yours,
A Black Man

Courage

The ability to do the things you do is unparalleled.
Your story should be that of legend,
Yet, it remains untold
Even by those that know who you are.

Courage is the choice to face your demons.
No matter the form they come,
And demons have haunted you since time began.

I've seen the struggling mother.
Lost in a world where she was thirsty for love.
Hungry with a desire to be better,
To do better for the children she birthed.
She moved from place to place trying to find stability.
A place to call home,
To keep her youth warm.
Deep down she bleeds tears,
Wanting to provide so much without having a dime.
She never gave up....
Accomplished all her dreams,

And became an unsung hero to her now grown children.

I held the hand of a woman,
That was misunderstood.
Guarded with walls that only God could get through.
She trusted no one,
Not even herself.
For history showed that the only reason people get close,
Is to stab you in the back.
She was betrayed by love,
From friends and family alike.
Broken vows and empty promises were all that remained.
She was down on herself,
Not knowing what would come next.
But she took the time and began to see life in a new light.
Once she took that first step in trusting herself,
Her path was enlightened,
And her latter days are blessed beyond compare.

I felt her memories,

Her life flashed before my eyes as she spoke,
Words that made her lips quiver.
Shame dawned on her face as she put her story on display.
I was tongue tied as she explained how she was bound.
Chills went through my spine when she said she was beaten.
Tears flowed from our eyes,
When she said she felt guilty while being robbed of her innocence.
She took the blame,
Though it wasn't hers to have.
She healed the scars,
But was left with a bruise that haunts her.
Today she stands strong,
Resilient,
Though she was left abused.
Her story is told to let others know they aren't alone.
And they too will rise with the morning sun.

You see this?
This is the story of legend

You are Brave!
You are Strong!

You are Powerful!

Adversity may cause you to stumble,
But you do not fall,
You do not break.
Courage is not what you have,
It's who you are!

Stand on it!
Stand by it!
And I will continue to stand by you.

I admire your consistency,
Humbled by your presence
And encouraged by your excellence.

Sincerely Yours,
A Black Man.

Ethereal

You are too perfect for this world

By definition, you are amazing.
You are the reason the sun rises.
Its rays intensify on you, to reflect the true beauty of your skin.
Your presence is a present.
A true gift to those who are blessed enough to encounter you.

Truly magnificent.
No words have been formulated to match how divine you are.
Even God said damn because of how fine you are.
You were crafted with the recipe of his excellence.

As it stands,
You are the breath of fresh air I can't wait to inhale.
The fire that ignites my soul and warms my heart.
Your smile is the nuclear deterrent that brings peace.
Peace of mind and peace to me.

Being connected to you, ties me to forever.

You are the foundation, formation, and preserver of my legacy.

These words don't do you justice,

But I hope they affirm that you are everything and more.

I am in awe of your greatness.

I bow humbly in reverence to you

Sincerely Yours,
A Black Man

Conferrer

You have already been known as an enhancer.

Turning groceries into meals,

A house into a home

And a seed into a child.

But it goes deeper than that.

You are the gift that keeps on giving.

Since your conception,
You've had the ability to change man and mankind.

Look at your history,

You've transformed jesters into royalty.

No man has become King without a Queen.

The reason we have princes and princesses,

Is because you crown them at birth.

The way we become rich is not through monetary instruments,

But through the love you give so effortlessly.

You are the world's most valuable asset.

And there is no contesting that.

Heaven on Earth exists because you are here.
Life would be lifeless without you.

Darkness would implode without your presence.

I Thank God and I Thank you,

For being such a wonderful gift.

Sincerely Yours,

A Black Man

As You Are

Sometimes I shake my head at you,
Wondering why you do the things you do.
Random gestures that are awkward turn into laughter.

Maybe it's the way you can't keep still when you talk,
Throwing hand signs with every word that you speak.
Knowing they have nothing to do with what you say,
But hope they add emphasis to your speech.

How about the way you place your food,
Making sure "nothing" touches another item
And if it does, you throw the whole plate away.

Maybe it's the way you cuddle.
Wanting to be underneath me literally
Digging your head into my armpit and sniffing,
Then releasing a breath of relief.

How about your laugh,

How it's just so loud and high pitched,
It's like you are trying to get everyone's attention,
But that's just how you laugh.

Maybe it's the way you frustrate me,
Eating all my food and won't touch your own.
And if I try and taste yours, you get an entire attitude.
Or maybe it's how you're a whole adult
And only order from the kid's menu.

Maybe it's your innocence,
How you look at every Disney Children's movie,
And get excited as if it was specifically made for you.

Maybe it's how you find comfort in my clothes,
And stake claim to everything that belongs to me.
Now I must borrow what used to be mine.

No matter what your quirk is,

It's still makes you uniquely you

And for that I will always love it,

The way I love you,

Sincerely Yours,
A Black Man

Arise

You have been the recipient of too much pain,
Dealing with individuals who shackle your mind in lies and deceit.
Imprisoning your body in bruises and bondage.
Misfortune has a tendency of revealing itself as the only card left in your hand.

Yet, you stand strong!

You have become accustomed to despair,
Because it's a look that you see in your reflection.
Days with no tears seem like dreams you don't want to awake from.
Nightmares are your new normal because of what you've been through.

But they can't break you!

His fist have been unwelcomed visitors in the love you once shared.
Matrimony has become polyamory,
Which are circumstances that were never agreed upon.

He left you with a child he said he would never leave,
And forced you to become the father you were never meant to be.
You've been stabbed in the back so much that it looks like you've had multiple spinal surgeries.

You have been the victim,
You have played the fool,
But just as a Phoenix arises from the ashes,
You will arise from the debris they tried to bury you in.

TODAY IS THE DAY YOU APOLOGIZE TO YOURSELF!

For allowing yourself to be treated in such manners.
For not valuing the beautiful being that you truly are.
Make a promise to yourself to be better to you,

And I will do the same.

I extend my hand to you.
With a promise of truth.

To never withhold what you deserve,
And to fuel the fire that burns bright in you.
I'm empathic to your circumstances.
I admire you for continuing to push
forward,
Even when you have more reasons to
succumb to the strain of your situation

My heart pours out to you,
And is open for you

Sincerely Yours,
A Black Man

<u>Sensational</u>

You are the truest depiction of exquisite.

Compiled of the most magnificent things the eyes can see.

You accentuate everything that is good in the world.

You are the perfect amalgam.

A combination of heaven, love, happiness and splendor in human form.

You are the fantasy,

Both romantically and sexually.

The key to unlocking the gift of true love.

The final destination of where lust and passion intertwine.

Hearts and minds open to you,

The kiss of your lips hypnotizes the senses,

Causing the body to fall in alignment with whatever you desire.

I'm elated to be in your presence.

If you truly believe in God,

Then you have an understanding of how the order in which things were created.

The light,

The Sky and Ocean,

The World,

Sun, Moon and Stars

The Birds and Animals

And His Masterpiece, which is you.

His most magnificent creation that he needed rest to observe.

I will follow his lead and observe you too.

Taking notice of the sway of your hips when you walk.

Looking as if you're dancing to the rhythm of my heart.

The glistening of your skin from the sun's gaze.

Adding the perfect filter to an already unblemished image.

It doesn't get any better!

Wanting the full experience of you,

I inhale deeply,

Getting lost in your aroma.

The sweetest sensations lie in your scent.

Feelings of benevolence taking possession of me

Without touching me,

You uplift me.

In encouragement and in prayer.

Your words to Gods ears,

Is how I've been blessed my entire life.

You make every moment worthwhile.

Capturing one memory with you,

Is enough to last me 1000 lifetimes.

And with every thought I have of you,

You will never die,

You will be etched in the world for an eternity,
Through my words,
And my love

Sincerely Yours,
A Black Man.

Remember Your Worth

I shed a tear for every piece of pain that he caused you

Unfortunately, he was too blind to see the truly remarkable person you are.

All you wanted was time and attention

And you sacrificed yourself for it.

Giving love to someone who was undeserving of it.

Someone that stopped putting forth any effort. Unworthy of your time and efforts.

Images remain vivid in my mind, reliving circumstances that you never should have been a part of.

Healing bruises and scars that should have never been placed upon your heart.

All you wanted was an unbreakable bond and everlasting relationship.

But what you got was far from what you deserved.

Please,

Understand and believe whole-heartedly that you are worth so much more!!

The tarnished relationships do not lessen your value because of their lack of effort.

From the husband that lost sight of God's Gift,

To the father that let his daughter wonder if she was ever good enough.

Love is what you are owed

And you should not belittle yourself or beg for something that's befitting.

They will soon come to notice that they lost more than love and will miss you dearly

You are the key:

To the kingdom,

To happiness,

And to life

The love you so desperately gave,

Give it to yourself and watch it come back in abundance.

And I will do my part to make sure you feel that love as well.

You are Precious,
You are Worthwhile,
And you are Laudable

Sincerely Yours,
A Black Man

Astounding

What a wonderful woman you are!

Simply Amazing!!

I am honored,

Yet undeserving, to be able to speak your name.

Your nobility is beyond contestability.

The characteristics and values that you possess should be engraved in every being.

Your grace is a blessing

Since I've known you,
You have demonstrated a strength that is unmatched.

What you've endured,

What you have overcome

Words can't be formed to express my sentiments or the gratitude I have for you.

You are the pillar of the family.

The foundation of love.

Even when losing everything,
Still finding a way and having the faith to push on.

Continuously giving everything to those you hold dear,

Even when you feel that you have nothing left.

You have been given plenty of reasons to turn your back against it all.

But still you stand firm and welcome all with open arms.

Being the mother to infidelity.

Giving more than the ones that conceived the child.

Treating and providing for them as if they were your own.

Being mature enough to recognize their innocence and not hold them accountable for something they were only a result of. Truly exceptional,

Having every right to be pretentious,

Yet having the humility to stay humble.

Always sacrificing yourself for the sake of others.

You are the personification of God's grace and love.

Again,

Enough can't be said about how truly remarkable you are.

I'm thankful and grateful to know you

I appreciate everything you are!

And all that you've done.

With Love,

Sincerely Yours,
A Black Man

Here I Stand

I hope these words find your heart,
To kiss the bruises that have been left.

I hope they glue the ties that have been severed between us.

The burden that has been placed on your shoulders should not be yours to bear alone.

The constant mistreatment and abuse remain inhumane.

The scrutiny and ridicule have left enough contusions for a lifetime

And as a man,
I admit I played my part in adding to those scars.

I've stood and watched you fight,

You've been stripped of your clothes and demoralized
You've been sexualized and objectified when you are so much more.

The rights you so earned,

Better yet deserved.
Have been overturned

Everything is trying to crumble and fall at your feet.

But you can stand on the fact that I'm here with you. Hell, you can stand on my back if you must.

I will stay silent and listen to anything you need.

I will stand in front of you and take the stones that are cast at you.

I will stand beside you to support you through it all.

And I will be behind you to enforce and promote you from hence forth.
I hope to honor your wishes and demands.

I will fight alongside you, as you have with me for eons

I got you,

I'm with you,

And I'm for you.

Sincerely Yours,

A Black Man

<u>Graceful</u>

How do you maintain the mental capacity to deal with continued ignorance?

In the beginning you explained,
"Err on the side of caution!!"
Because the day you're lost,
It will be regretted.
And your warning wasn't heeded.

There was an attempt to wound you emotionally,
Damage your intellect,
And deceive what you knew to be true.

Which is that they were unworthy of you.

Regardless of their actions against you,
The best vengeance you could fathom,
Was the time they no longer had with you.

You rose above,
Never spoke ill of their character.
Though they tried again and again to defame you.

Truth is,
Their misery comes from the words they spoke.
The fact that they are no longer gifted with your presence,
Is why their lies cut them deeper than they do you.

This is a testament to your Grace!
It's easy to have an eye for an eye mentality,
To belittle or demean someone who has done wrong to you.

Yet still,
You show that revenge can be a dish best served warm,
By showing compassion and bestowing well wishes upon those who opposed you.

Understanding that knocking someone down doesn't make you bigger,
But elevating above their pettiness and ignorance does make you better.

You embody Sophistication,
Exuberate Excellence,
And Exemplify Grace

Continue to model integrity and goodness,

As you are mesmerizing because of it.

Sincerely Yours,
A Black Man

Rebirth of a Queen

I've watched as you've had men come in and out of your life,

As if they were passing by only to be a reflection of pain that would haunt your memories, terrorize your reality,

and secure your insecurities,

Letting them reap the benefits of your innocence

Releasing any presence of self-confidence, you may have had.

I'm here to tell you that you are not that woman.

Don't let his mistakes take shape in who you are.

You are not an empty vessel,

So don't let people fill you with whatever they desire.

You're created from passion,

Designed by divinity

And manifested by greatness.

Let that fuel your fire.

Those that try to extinguish the essence of your beauty

Will only feel the heat of your flame

Because the fire that burns,

Is bright and deep within.

You're worth more than what you're told.

Exist as if your heart is encrusted in gold,

and your soul is formed by blue diamonds

Then stand on the fact that you are still invaluable

Let your aura define the elegance within

Let yesterday be the death of the woman that was,

And today be the resurrection of the queen that is You!!!

Sincerely Yours,

A Black Man

My Apologies

As a man,
I carry the weight of the world on my shoulders.

Constantly being criticized and scrutinized for the color of my skin.
Oppressed by others because they understand the true nature of my power even more than myself.

With that burden comes pain,
And that pressure tends to get unbearable.

Unfortunately, those things trickle down,
And my frustrations come down on you
Which isn't fair.

So, this is my apology to you.

You are not the reason I cheated.
You were the scapegoat,
That way I didn't have to check myself.
I was not man enough to own my mistakes,
Nor was I able to admit to you that I was wrong.

I am the blame for your insecurities and trust issues,
You are not to blame for my infidelity.

I chose to leave you alone,
Though you needed me to help raise our child.

I didn't give you an option to live out your dreams
Because I wasn't man enough to accept my responsibilities.

It was easier for me to run,
Then to grow and mature.
How am I strong enough to raise another man's child,
But won't do the same for my own?

My weakness is why I hit you.
I raised my hand in anger toward you,
And that sting will stay in my soul forever.
Whether I was hurt or livid,
You never deserved that outcome.

Society dictates that we are worthless,
And I added to that by treating you less than.

Knowing you're worth more than I can even comprehend.
I was blind to the fact that I was holding you back,
And making you fight more than you needed to.

I created the scars,
And the walls that you built.
Causing you self-doubt by constantly defaming your character.
Fed you lies,
Leaving you full of deception and fabrications.
When you should be satiated with love,
Adoration and reverence.

I'm here to tell you that

I WAS WEAK!
I WAS A COWARD!
I WAS WRONG!
For all that I have done to you.

I apologize for leaving you,
A single mother,
Battered and bruised,
With no true sense of who you truly are.

You deserve and will receive better from me

My deepest apologies

Sincerely Yours,
A Black Man

Treasure

Invaluable, Vital,
The essence of life and love.

Altruistic, Nurturing,
Essential to Everyday.

You are the truth,
Effervescent,
And nourishing to the soul.

How does one quantify the worth of
something so precious and priceless?
How do you define one that is boundless?
How do you confine light in darkness?

You Can't!!

Still, I hope to plant these words,
To inhabit your heart,
And dwell in your mind
For as long as time will allow.

You have Power!
You have Purpose!
You are Greatness!

Limitless devotion and care,
Is what you've demonstrated for others.

And reciprocity should be given in abundance for what you've sacrificed.

You are the fine line between a dream and reality.
The resurrection of beauty and decency.

Her magnetism attracts benevolence,
Bringing serenity to the enraged.

Despite what may have been spewed about you,
And how your name gets dragged through the dirt.

You are the Hidden Gem in plain sight.

A True Treasure,

Sincerely Yours,
A Black Man

Refuge

When it comes to escaping, feeling comforted, and feeling safe

There is no place I'd rather be than your arms.

In the world we live in,

There is so much danger,

So much pain,

So much anguish...

And you are the only one that has the ability to deliver us from it

Even if only for a moment.

The power of your touch is immense.

And the love in that touch is bottomless.

You inculcate confidence, peace, and security into the lives you're a part of.

You are the safe haven,

The sanctuary of hope

And I say thank you for being here.

Without your direction,

Without your empathy and understanding,

Hell, Without you

I would be lost.

Again, I say thank you

For your guidance,

For being the everlasting light in the dark skies.

And being the keeper and preserver of my heart

From this point,
Until time ends

I strive to reciprocate all that you have given tenfold

Sincerely Yours,
A Black Man

A Sneak Peek into what's next....

These Eyes

These eyes…………

These eyes do not lie to you.

The misconceptions that have been created by your mind

Will not hold if you look into my eyes.

Many things have been seen through these eyes.

Love. Hate.. Life…Death….

Have all been seen through these eyes.

These eyes………..

These eyes have lived through transgressions.

They've seen the tears of a mother as she was beaten,

By a man that "loved" her.

Kept Secrets of infidelity on behalf of both parties.

These eyes…..

They've seen life come into this world

And could see the innocence in it.

They've seen laughter and happiness,

Even if only for a brief instance.

They have seen life gone in an instant.

Brains splattered all over the pavement,

Watched a mother bury her child that was gone too soon.

These eyes tell no lies

But are you ready to be exposed to the secrets inside.

About the Author

Author Darryl Johnson originates from Kansas City, KS and graduated from Wyandotte High School. Being from this inner city, most if not all, are expected to only be statics in the world we live in. Despite what society set against him, he rose to new heights, achieving a bachelor's degree from Strayer University. When asked what legacy do you want to leave behind? Darryl simply stated that he just wants the people he loves to know that he loves them, and to feel that from him at all times.

www.ingramcontent.com/pod-product-compliance
Lightning Source LLC
Chambersburg PA
CBHW031411040426
42444CB00005B/511